CROCODILES

— BUILT FOR THE HUNT —

by Tammy Gagne

Consultant: Dr. Jackie Gai, D

Raintree is an imprint of Capstone Global Library Limited, a company incorporated in England
and Wales having its registered office at 264 Banbury Road, Oxford, OX2 7DY – Registered
company number: 6695582

www.raintree.co.uk
myorders@raintree.co.uk

Editorial Credits
Brenda Haugen, editor; Juliette Peters, designer; Tracy Cummins,
media researcher; Katy LaVigne, production specialist

Printed and bound in China.

ISBN 978 1 474 70197 6 (hardback)
19 18 17 16 15
10 9 8 7 6 5 4 3 2 1

ISBN 978 1 474 70204 1 (paperback)
20 19 18 17 16
10 9 8 7 6 5 4 3 2

British Library Cataloguing in Publication Data
A full catalogue record for this book is available from the British Library.

Photo Credits
Getty Images: Cultura RM/Lou Coetzer, 5, DEA/C.DANI-I.JESKE, 7, Federico Veronesi, 20, Ian
Waldie, 6, Mike Korostelev, 18, Peter Walton Photography, 1, Sylvain Cordier, 19, Victoria Stone
& Mark Deeble, 10; iStockphoto: Byronsdad, 8; Shutterstock: alexnika, 12, apiguide, 15, Audrey
Snider-Bell, Cover, dangdumrong, 16, Ian Scott, 11, Back Cover, Johan Swanepoel, 3, konmesa, 2,
17, Mogens Trolle, 13, Nila Newsom, 21, pashabo, Design Element, Stuart G Porter, 9.

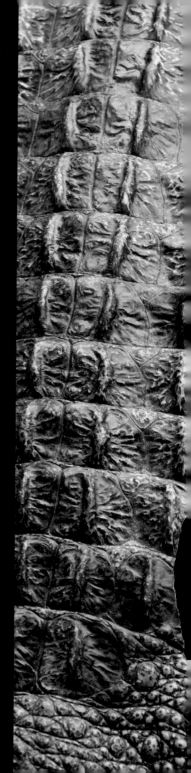

CONTENTS

OUT OF NOWHERE

A zebra strolls towards a river for a drink. A hungry crocodile waits in the water. When the zebra lowers its head, the powerful **predator** springs into action. The crocodile grabs its helpless **prey**.

Crocodiles are deadly predators. They hunt many types of prey, including small **mammals**, fish, deer and birds.

FACT

Crocodiles also hunt some very large animals. They can even kill a small hippopotamus that weighs about 2,268 kilograms (5,000 pounds). That's heavier than an average car!

predator animal that hunts other animals for food

prey animal hunted by another animal for food

mammal warm-blooded animal that breathes air; mammals have hair or fur; female mammals feed milk to their young

BIG AND STRONG

Saltwater crocodiles are the largest crocodiles. They can grow up to 6.7 metres (22 feet) long. This **species** uses its size and strength to overpower prey.

Nile crocodiles are smaller, but are still big and strong. They grow to about 5 metres (16 feet) long. Like saltwater crocodiles, Nile crocodiles use their size and power for hunting. But Nile crocodiles also eat dead animals left by other predators.

FACT

A saltwater crocodile has the strongest bite in the animal kingdom. It can crush the skull of a fully-grown water buffalo.

species group of animals with similar features

ATTACK!

Crocodiles can run faster than humans. But they do not waste energy chasing prey on land. Crocodiles wait for prey to come to them. As soon as a prey animal moves within reach, a crocodile **lunges** at it. Moving through water uses less energy. Crocodiles often swim after fish and turtles.

FACT

Some crocodiles have thin **snouts** that can grab prey from underwater holes. Their snouts act like giant tweezers to grab small prey such as shrimp.

lunge move forwards quickly and suddenly

snout long front part of an animal's head; the snout includes the nose, mouth and jaws

A FAST SWIMMER

Crocodiles move quickly when chasing prey in the water. The Nile crocodile can swim 29 kilometres (18 miles) per hour. That is about three times faster than an Olympic swimmer!

A crocodile can hold its breath a long time. A crocodile waiting for prey can stay under water for up to two hours.

GRAB AND DRAG

Crocodiles have 60 to 75 razor-sharp teeth. They use their teeth for catching and holding onto prey. After getting a firm grip on prey, crocodiles drag their prey under water and drown it.

FACT

When a crocodile loses a tooth, another tooth grows in its place. A crocodile may have 3,000 teeth in its lifetime!

SHARP SENSES

Crocodiles have sharp senses to help them to hunt. They can see well both on land and in water. They also have excellent hearing. Crocodiles can hear many sounds that humans cannot. Crocodiles have large **lobes** in their brains that help them to smell nearby animals.

lobe curved or rounded part of an organ such as the brain

A THICK SKIN

Tough scales called **scutes** cover most of a crocodile's body. These bony scales act like a suit of armour. Even if prey tries to bite back, a crocodile will almost always win the fight.

FACT

Crocodiles are always growing new scutes. As new scutes grow, the old ones fall out.

scute wide scale

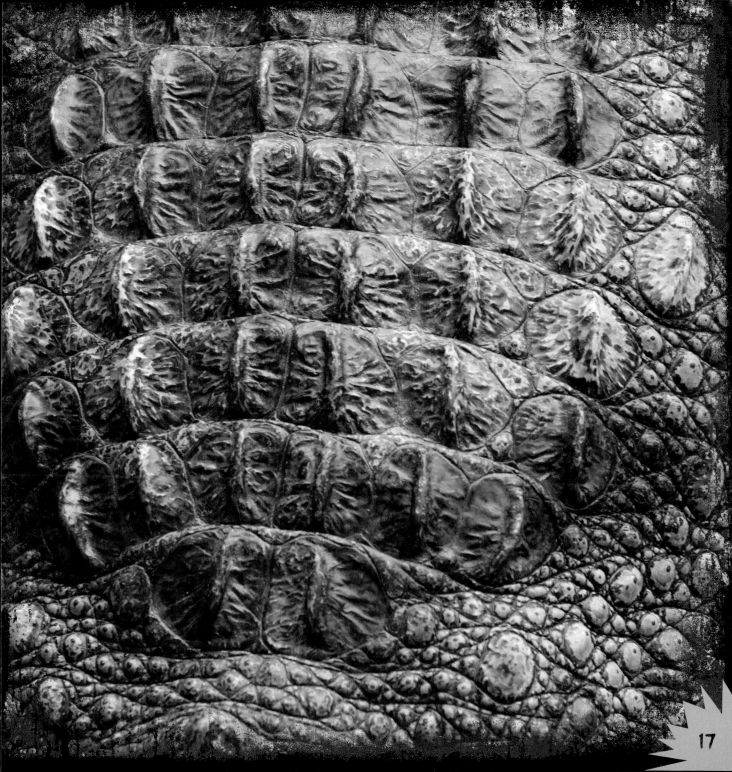

BY LEAPS AND BOUNDS

   Crocodiles are skilled jumpers. They can leap high up into the air. They use their strong tails to push themselves into the air. Many crocodiles catch birds this way.

EVENING MEALS

Crocodiles are **nocturnal**. They do most of their hunting at night. Crocodiles often sleep in the daytime sun. But they are always on alert. A crocodile can go from snoozing to snapping in just seconds!

nocturnal active at night and resting during the day

AMAZING BUT TRUE!

Crocodiles can go without food for a long time. Most crocodiles eat only about 50 times each year. Crocodiles can survive for an entire year without eating anything at all!

GLOSSARY

lobe curved or rounded part of an organ such as the brain

lunge move forwards quickly and suddenly

mammal warm-blooded animal that breathes air; mammals have hair or fur; female mammals feed milk to their young

nocturnal active at night and resting during the day

predator animal that hunts other animals for food

prey animal hunted by another animal for food

scute wide scale

snout long front part of an animal's head; the snout includes the nose, mouth and jaws

species group of animals with similar features

READ MORE

Amazing Predators (Animal Superpowers), John Townsend (Raintree, 2013)

Crocodile vs Wildebeest (Predator vs Prey), Mary Meinking Chambers (Raintree, 2012)

Reptiles (Animal Classification), Angela Royston (Raintree, 2015)

WEBSITES

www.bbc.co.uk/nature/life/Nile_crocodile

Learn more about Nile crocodiles.

www.bbc.co.uk/nature/life/Crocodylus

Learn more about crocodiles that live in Africa, Asia, Australia and the Americas.

www.crocodilesoftheworld.co.uk

Learn about the Crocodiles of the World crocodile conservation and education centre. You can even plan your visit!

COMPREHENSION QUESTIONS

1. Does a crocodile's body help to protect it during a fight? How?

2. Look at the fact box on page 8. In what other ways might a long, thin snout be useful to a crocodile?

INDEX